Religious Experience

by Wendy Dossett

Series Editor: Roger J. Owen

Note about dates

This book uses the abbreviations CE and BCE for Common Era and Before the Common Era. In some books you will find AD (Anno Domini) for CE and BC (Before Christ) for BCE. The actual years are the same, only the tag is different.

Credits

The author and publishers are grateful to the following for permission to reproduce copyright photographs in this book:
Mary Evans Picture Library p.7 (bottom); Rex p.7 (top), p.14; iStockphoto p.9; Dolf Hartsuiker, from his book 'Sadhus: Holy Men of India', published by Thames & Hudson p.20.

Every effort has been made to contact copyright holders of material reproduced in this publication. Any omission will be rectified in subsequent printings if notice is given to the publisher. While the information in this publication is believed to be true and accurate at the date of going to press, neither the author nor the publisher can accept any legal responsibility for any errors or omissions that may be made.

Roger J. Owen, Series Editor

Roger J. Owen was Head of RE in a variety of schools for thirty years, as well as being a Head of Faculty, advisory teacher for primary and secondary RE, Section 23 Inspector and 'O' Level and GCSE Chief Examiner. Author of seventeen educational titles, he is currently an education consultant and WJEC Religious Studies AS and A2 Chair of Examiners.

Published by UWIC Press
UWIC, Cyncoed Road,
Cardiff CF23 6XD
cgrove@uwic.ac.uk
029 2041 6515

ISBN 978-1-905617-12-8

Design by the info group
Picture research by Glyn Saunders Jones
Printed by MWL Digital

Sponsored by the Welsh Assembly Government
© 2006 Wendy Dossett

Religious Experience

by Wendy Dossett

Series Editor: Roger J. Owen

Contents

Tackling the Topic

Religious Experience is a most fascinating area to study. Religious experiences are diverse and raise many interesting questions. Are such experiences merely an aspect of ordinary human life, caused by a certain pattern of brain activity and interpreted in a particular way due to prior belief, culture and environment? Or is religious experience compelling evidence for the existence of a Supreme Being? What impact does having a religious experience make on an individual?

That the study of religious authority is a crucial part of your A Level course is evident from the fact that 40% of A2 marks, 20% of the entire A Level, are allocated to it. Indeed, from 2010 onwards it will be allocated 50% of the A2 marks and 25% of the entire A level. It is a unique part of your course because it is only through this theme that you demonstrate your skills in linking different areas of Religious Studies.

What you need to do

To achieve the highest grade in the synoptic assessment you need to demonstrate:
- knowledge and understanding of religious experience in at least two distinct areas (e.g. Buddhism and Philosophy of Religion);
- knowledge and understanding of the connections between relevant elements of these areas;
- ability to relate these areas to a relevant aspect of human experience (e.g. awareness of the numinous);
- ability to make relevant comparisons and contrasts between these areas;
- appropriate use of technical language and terminology;
- knowledge, understanding and analysis of relevant views of scholars and/or schools of thought;
- ability to support arguments with appropriate examples from these areas;
- ability to evaluate different points of view and reach an appropriate conclusion;
- high quality of language including clarity in expression and coherence in structure.

N.B. From 2010, synopticity is required in all A2 modules and may be demonstrated by exploring connections between elements of a single area of study, not necessarily two or more areas. Therefore, comments in this chapter about two or more areas may be ignored after 2009.

What help to expect

You can expect a reasonable amount of guidance from your teacher. Indeed, usually the role of the teacher is vital to student success. Teachers want you to do well and are there to teach relevant topics and stimulate interest in them.

Your teacher should:
- tell you about the pre-examination information and advise you what key aspects of religious experience to concentrate on;

- make you aware of the assessment demands of the level descriptors, the basis on which your examination answer is marked;
- suggest and provide some appropriate resources;
- assist you in planning and organising your work;
- check on your progress, reading written drafts and discussing ideas and issues which emerge from your own studies.

What is not legitimate is for someone other than you to produce an ideal response and for you and other students to learn and reproduce it under examination conditions. This malpractice clearly hampers the thinking of abler candidates, disadvantages weaker candidates when material is not understood properly and penalises all candidates when that person has inadvertently introduced material deemed by examiners to be irrelevant.

How to structure an essay on religious experience

A sound essay structure incorporates:

- a brief introduction
- accurate information
- a wide range of knowledge
- clear expression of ideas and understanding
- a variety of views
- examples in the main part of the essay
- evidence, analysis, perception and coherence in the conclusion.

Questions are normally structured in two parts. The first part tests your knowledge and understanding of a particular aspect of religious experience. The second tests your analytical, critical and evaluative skills. Analytical skills are shown when you point out the complexity and compare different aspects of an issue or argument and consider to what extent they are supported by evidence and/or logic. Critical skills are demonstrated when you identify and explain arguments for and against a viewpoint or controversial statement and make a reasoned judgement about the accuracy or validity of those arguments. Evaluative skills are similar and are evident when you review the strengths and weaknesses of a viewpoint or balance two or more opinions on an issue and conclude with a reasoned personal opinion.

A basic structure for an answer is as follows:

Introduction	placing question/response in context, including definition/clarification of key terms; proposed method of tackling question, including stating areas to be used in answering question.
Main part	clearly separate responses to each part of the question; each area of study examined in turn; each paragraph having one major point, usually stated in the opening sentence of the paragraph; remainder of the paragraph consisting of elaboration, illustration, examination and/or application of that point.
Conclusion	in part (a), comparison and contrast of different relevant concepts within the areas used; in part (b), analysis of different viewpoints followed by a reasoned personal viewpoint based on the evidence presented.

What to avoid

A-level examiners have been impressed with the breadth and depth of knowledge, degree of understanding and perception in analysis shown by many candidates when tackling questions on religious experience. However, the most prominent common weakness of the performance of candidates in recent years has been failure to demonstrate clearly connections between areas being examined. Amazingly, some candidates make no effort at all to make connections. Others concentrate on one area with literally only one or two brief references to a second area.

However extensive or excellent the material, an essay will be ungraded if it does not contain any explicit reference to two different areas of study. In such a case the candidate has failed to draw together synoptically knowledge, understanding and skills. Where there is very little reference to a second area of study, the maximum award could be grade D, but is more likely to be grade E. It would depend on whether the quality of that reference was considered basic or only superficial.

Where the second area of study used in an answer is valid in its own right but is not within the content of the Religious Studies A-level Specification (e.g. sociology, anthropology, spiritualism), the maximum award is Level 3 – just over half marks. This is because candidates are demonstrating skills but not knowledge and understanding learned in different elements of their course of study, which is a requirement. However, where valid material from an area or areas outside the Specification content is included *in addition* to that from two areas of study within the Specification, no such restriction would apply. It should also be noted that identical perspectives/areas do not have to be referred to in responses to both parts of a question on religious experience.

How to make connections

Explicit *comment* on connections between areas of study is essential for the award of Level 5 in part (a) of the essay. Such comment needs to be diverse, extensive or significant to warrant higher marks within the Level. One brief or banal comment would only justify the lowest mark within the Level. Making connections is achieved most impressively when candidates point out comparisons and contrasts throughout their answer. However, this is a complex task. Alternatively, in a structured essay, a substantial concluding paragraph in response to each part-question highlighting main similarities and differences of relevant belief, concept, experience or practice between the areas is often adequate.

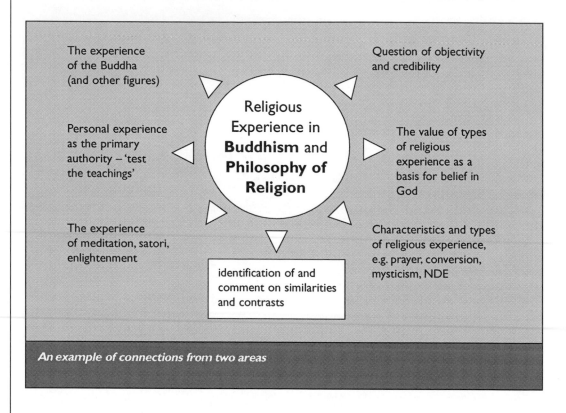

The experience of the Buddha (and other figures)

Personal experience as the primary authority – 'test the teachings'

The experience of meditation, satori, enlightenment

Religious Experience in **Buddhism** and **Philosophy of Religion**

Question of objectivity and credibility

The value of types of religious experience as a basis for belief in God

Characteristics and types of religious experience, e.g. prayer, conversion, mysticism, NDE

identification of and comment on similarities and contrasts

An example of connections from two areas

You should be aware that the use of examples from a different area does not constitute 'comment'. For example, if mysticism (Philosophy of Religion) is merely illustrated by the kabbalah (Judaism) that would not be deemed to constitute 'comment'. However, if a contrast was pointed out between forms of mysticism found in different religions, say the kabbalah and mystic experiences of Julian of Norwich (Christianity), then that would be valid comment on connections between areas of study.

Remember, the demand to comment on connections does not apply in part (b) where the emphasis is on the contribution of areas, not the connections between them.[1]

Writing task

Choose **two** areas of study. Brainstorm all the aspects of religious experience you can think of to be found in these two areas and produce a spider diagram for each area. Then create a mind map showing the links between them.

---

[1]Many of the general principles in this chapter are found in 'Solving the Synoptic Problem' by Roger J. Owen in **Newyddion AG/RE News**, Issue 65, Spring 2003, p.4 and 'Achieving Synoptic Success' by Roger J. Owen in **Dialogue**, Issue 21, November 2003, pp. 27-30.

Religious Experience: the Field

Introduction

Throughout history, religious or spiritual experience has been reported by human beings all over the world. It is arguable that many of the world's religions were founded on the religious experience of an individual; for example, Guru Nanak (Sikhism) the Buddha (Buddhism), or the Prophet Muhammad (Islam). As well as individual figures, the experiences of significant groups are also often seen as foundational; for example, the rishis or 'seers' who wrote the Vedas (Hinduism), or the Israelites (Judaism), or the Apostles in the Early Church (Christianity).

In addition to these founder figures there are countless numbers of celebrated religious people, or religious 'virtuosos' as Max Weber describes them, who figure in the histories and literatures of the religions, like the saints and mystics of Christianity and the self-realised Gurus of the Indian Traditions. These figures are celebrated for their profound experiences which have informed their teachings.

Moreover, it is sometimes forgotten in the study of religions that ordinary contemporary human beings in many, if not all, cultures of the world report that they have had religious experiences of a wide variety of kinds. From spectacular visions of religious figures, near death experiences and dramatic conversions or healings, to the simple sense of assurance that 'all is well', ordinary people, even people who would not describe themselves as religious, report such experiences with surprising frequency. It is possible also to talk about the 'experience of religion', referring not to a separate 'event', but simply to the individual's ongoing engagement with the beliefs and practices of her religion. Visiting a place of worship, for example, is 'an experience.'

For the student of religion these experiences pose a great many questions. For example:

- Are religious experiences veridical? To put it another way, are they experiences of anything real? Are they best explained as 'emotional' or 'aesthetic' experiences rather than religious experiences?

- Religious experiences are often described as beyond words (ineffable). If this is so, how can they be communicated? How can they be tested (if they can)?

- Can someone be 'deluded' about an experience that they think they have had?

- What happens if a religious believer has an experience which does not conform to the teachings of their religion?

- How important is 'experience' in religion, compared to other sources of authority such as priests/rabbis/gurus, or sacred scriptures?

Discussion task

Discuss your responses to these questions.

Writing task

Write down any other 'questions' about religious experience which you may have.

For Ninian Smart, the UK's first Professor of Religious Studies, experience was one important feature of religions amongst six others. In his book *The World's Religions* (1989), he describes the dimensions of religion as follows:

- **The practical and ritual dimension**
  Smart describes this as worship, preaching, sacrifice, yoga, prayers and so on;
- **The experiential and emotional dimension**
  The personal and collective experience of 'the Absolute';
- **The narrative and mythic dimension**
  The stories of religions, for example about founders such as Moses, Jesus, Muhammad or the Buddha, or myths about creation, or good and evil;
- **The doctrinal and philosophical dimension**
  The beliefs about the nature of reality and the role of the human being;
- **The ethical and legal dimension**
  The code of conduct by which it is expected believers will live, for example the Eightfold Path or the Ten Commmandments or the Shari'a;
- **The social and institutional dimension**
  The community which preserves the beliefs and practices of the religion, such as the Church, or Umma, or Sangha;
- **The material dimension**
  Buildings, works of art etc., or even the features of the natural world, for example Mt Sinai; or, in some religions, any mountain, stream, tree or rock.

Smart argues (p21) that all religions have these dimensions, (though admittedly in a minority of cases some may be so weak as to be virtually absent; for example non-literate societies who don't have formal doctrines). He sees the dimensions as tools for giving balanced descriptions of religions as they exist in the world. Clearly, the experiential dimension is important. He lists the visions of Muhammad, the conversion of Paul and the Enlightenment of the Buddha as 'seminal' events in human history.

However, he goes further to link the experiential with the 'emotional'. To illustrate this (p13) he points to the feelings, such as love, awe, peace, gratitude and hope, that people have in relation to their religious rituals and doctrines and myths, which give an experiential basis to their engagement with religion. He says that it is important when we are trying to understand a religion to 'enter in' to the feelings which it generates, and he describes experience as the 'food on which the other dimensions feed'. This shows the importance of the dimension of experience.

Writing task

Evaluate the role of experience in Smart's dimensions of religion.

How are religious experiences different from ordinary experiences?

This is a question which can be explored from a number of different angles, and there is no clear cut answer. Some might say that religious experiences are different because they involve the experience of an invisible world, not accessible by the senses. However, not all experiences which are described as religious are like this. People might say, for example, that their experience of nature, or their experience of giving birth, was a religious experience. In their descriptions there might be no reference to anything beyond the senses, no mysterious power or force. However, they say it is religious because of its profound *effect* on their lives. Are such experiences 'religious experiences'? What would religious institutions say about these experiences?

Is a near death experience in which someone feels they are floating upwards, seeing a life-review and meeting deceased relatives, a *religious* experience? It contains no reference to God, or to any religious beliefs. The person who has this experience may not be religious, either before or after the experience.

A religious person might have an experience, for example a vision of the Virgin Mary. Are we to say that this is *in fact* an experience of the Virgin Mary? Or could the person have been interpreting some natural phenomenon (an actual woman in their field of vision) in that way because of a prior belief in the Virgin? Is this a religious experience, or an ordinary experience with a religious interpretation?

Pilgrims at Lourdes

How common are religious experiences?

Sir Alister Hardy

In 1969 a marine biologist, zoologist and Oxford Professor, Sir Alister Hardy, began work collecting religious experiences from the general public. He advertised in newspapers and elsewhere asking for anyone who had been 'conscious of, or influenced by, a power, whether they call it God or not' to write to him about it. This is known as 'the Hardy Question'.

He had an overwhelming response, and founded the Religious Experience Research Unit, which is now known as the Religious Experience Research Centre (RERC). The RERC (which is based at the University of Wales, Lampeter) holds a unique archive of more than 6,000 accounts of religious or spiritual experience, sent in by members of the general public. Sir Alister's purpose had been to collect experiences and, as a scientist, to analyse them and categorise them into 'types'. He was a Darwinian evolutionist, but unlike

Sir Alister Hardy

many who dismissed religion, he argued that religious experience was a key feature of the survival of the species, since they made people stronger, gave them a sense of purpose and better relationships with others.

Researchers from all over the world continue to analyse the contents of Sir Alister's archive and draw conclusions about the nature of religious experience from it. One important finding has been the unexpected frequency of religious experience, or to put it another way, a surprisingly large number of people have them. In 1987 David Hay, who was a Director of the RERC, showed that at least 33% of the population would answer 'yes' to the 'Hardy Question'. Interestingly, he also showed that more women than men report having them, and those who had them were not always members of churches or religious traditions.[2] More recently he has argued that nowadays 76% are comfortable with reporting that they have had a spiritual experience.[3] This may be because it is becoming increasingly acceptable in our culture to speak about such experiences.

What triggers religious experiences?

Various studies have been done to see what triggers a religious experience. One of the most common triggers is a crisis of some kind. The most obvious of these is any religious experience which occurs around death. The Near Death Experience, where the recipient reports having experienced certain things whilst unconscious prior to resuscitation, is one such experience.

The classic NDE has certain features which are only triggered by proximity to clinical death. However, there are other religious experiences associated with death, such as Death Bed Visions, where a terminally ill person begins to see deceased relatives or other figures over a period of time prior to death. Furthermore, there are reports that someone who has come close to death or has in fact died, even though his or her loved ones are not aware of it, appears to them in a dream or vision, which seems to them at the time to have no meaning, until they discover that their loved one has indeed passed on.

One's own death, or the death of a close loved one, is a highly traumatic event, and it seems that this kind of crisis is frequently a trigger for some kind of experience that many would describe as religious. There are other, possibly equally traumatic, experiences in life that also trigger such experiences. People with mental illness or depression often report profound religious experiences which transform their lives. People suffering psychological breakdown in relation to loss of love, failed relationships, addiction, child-abuse, criminal behaviour, war and so on, also often report life-changing experiences which enable them to cope and which they describe in religious or spiritual terms.

Of course, philosophers and psychologists question the veracity of such experiences, often preferring to describe them in psychological or naturalistic terms. This will be discussed further in Chapter Four.

---

[2]David Hay, *Exploring Inner Space*, Oxford, Mowbray, 1987
[3]David Hay & Gordon Heald, 'Religion is good for you' *New Society*, April 17 1987, pp20-22

Other triggers may fall either inside or outside of religious categories. Many religious experiences occur during acts of formal or personal worship or meditation. Many of the Christian Mystics for example, lived lives dedicated completely to the practice of contemplative prayer, and their experiences arise out of that context. Ordinary believers often report a sense of awareness of the 'numinous' or holy, when attending a religious service in the synagogue or church, for example. Particular parts of a service might arouse that kind of feeling, for example the Eucharist or communion in some Christian Churches, or the Kaddish in the Synagogue, or the sharing of prashad in the Gurdwara or Mandir. The singing of hymns, psalms or religious songs, or the chanting of mantras or sutras, or the beat of a shamanic drum, often function as triggers. In fact in many religions the practice of communal singing or chanting is designed to bring about an altered state of consciousness in which a sense of the holy, sacred, or 'other' may be achieved. The same is true of communal prayers, or other communal activities, such as pilgrimage.

Research task

Drawing on any religions you have studied, make a list of religious activities which might entail or result in a religious experience.

Alternatively many people report that simply being in a holy place provides a trigger for some kind of experience. The experience of being alone in an empty cathedral, or sitting in front of a rupa (image or statue) of the Buddha in a meditation room, or being in the presence of the Guru Granth Sahib, in a particular frame of mind, can induce an experience of the sacred.

Outside of a religious context, many religious experiences are inspired by the natural world. Many ordinary people are moved by awesome scenic beauty, from Uluru (Ayres Rock) or Niagara Falls, to Snowdonia or the Yorkshire Moors. As well as such scenery, a simple, delicate wild flower or insect, or even the amazing complexity and beauty of the human body, have the power to trigger a different state of consciousness in people. For many it is impossible to see these aspects of our world and be unaware of the hand of the divine in their creation. For others awareness of the natural world brings about a sense of personal insignificance, combined with a sense of connectedness with, and dependence upon, the natural world. Some people have Out of Body Experiences, visions, or other types of quite spectacular experience triggered by the natural world. Others have a less dramatic but equally significant sense of the sacred, or of meaning.

The scenic beauty of Snowdonia

For the Romantic poets, for example, William Wordsworth, a profound sense of awareness of the natural world was so life-giving as to be religious in itself, such as is shown in these lines from *Tintern Abbey*

> *...And I have felt*
> *A presence that disturbs me with the joy*
> *Of elevated thoughts; a sense sublime*
> *Of something far more deeply interfused,*
> *Whose dwelling is the light of setting suns,*
> *And the round ocean and the living air.*
> *And the blue sky, and in the mind of man:*
> *A motion and a spirit, that impels*
> *All thinking things, all objects of all thought,*
> *And rolls through all things.*

Other triggers outside of the religious context include music, often classical music, but other genres too. Both listening or making, or even dancing to music are frequently triggers. In fact any kind of immersion in a creative activity can be a trigger.

Some, such as Timothy Leary and Aldous Huxley, have argued that the use of psychedelic (meaning 'mind opening') drugs (for example LSD, mescaline, psilocybin) can be triggers for religious experiences. Experiences while the brain has been chemically altered certainly have similarities with commonly reported features of religious experience. For example some users of psychedelic drugs report feelings of extreme happiness and well-being, the sense of being given the secrets of the universe, encounter with beings not of this world, the transcendence of time and space, a sense of unity and love.

Psychedelic drugs have historically been used, and in some religious traditions still are used, in order to bring about religious experiences. Soma, for example, was a psychoactive substance both used and worshipped in the ancient Vedic period of Hinduism. Peyote, a hallucinogenic mushroom, is used by many Native American tribes, and cannabis is used in a religious context by some Rastafarians.

The question of whether psychedelic experiences and religious experiences are the same is much debated by scholars. Most scholars argue, however, that because the effects of the psychedelic experience are not long-lived or life transforming, and there are few or no positive 'fruits' (and often many very negative ones such as addiction, personality breakdown and death), and also that they are experiences *induced* by outside means, rather than experiences which simply happen, that they cannot, except in a minority of cultural settings, be counted as religious experiences.

Types and Characteristics of Religious Experiences

Whilst it is always important to remember that religious experience refers just as much to the mundane experience of everyday religious life, there are some specific forms or types of religious experience which are often listed. These pose interesting problems for philosophers, to be discussed in Chapter 4.

Numerous writers have proposed their own 'typologies' of religious experiences, but of course it is important to remember that many experiences fall into more than one category at the same time. Peter Donovan (*Interpreting Religious Experience*) and Moojan Momen (*The Phenomenon of Religion*) use the following general typology, which was taken from the great philosopher and psychologist William James' seminal study of religious experience, *The Varieties of Religious Experience* (1902):

Regenerative experiences

This is the experience of a reality greater than the individual, which transforms and revitalizes them. An example of a regenerative experience would be a religious conversion, which involves a radical change in values and lifestyle, or the experience of a new hope, joy, or certainty, such as the feeling of being forgiven or healed, or simply finding a greater sense of purpose in life. A great many religious experiences are of this type.

Charismatic experiences

A charismatic experience involves the receiving of a 'gift', such as speaking in tongues, the ability to heal, or the power of prophecy. Charismatic experiences are found in many religions, with churches or movements particularly associated with such experiences (for example the Charismatic and Pentecostal Churches of Christianity worldwide) and in particular celebrated individuals such as Hindu gurus, shaykhs and pirs of the Islamic Sufi tradition, shamans and witchdoctors in primal religions.

Mystical experiences

The study of mystical experience is a huge field of scholarship. In its simplest form, mysticism is the direct experience of the divine. However, there are many different types of mystical experiences, amongst which three are common.

a) Apophatic experience

Many mystics from the world's religions describe their experience negatively, by saying what it is not. This is because words cannot describe what it is; it lies beyond language, it is ineffable. For example, Dionysus the Areopagite writes of his experience of God:

> 'The cause of all things is neither soul nor intellect; nor has it imagination, opinion, or reason, or intelligence, nor is it spoken or thought, . . . It is neither essence, nor eternity, nor time . . . not unity; not divinity or goodness; nor even spirit as we know it.'[1]

Consequently, a feature of much mystical experience is the idea of silence.

[1]James, Varieties, p402

b) Unitive experience

A very common feature of many reported mystical experiences is that the recipient feels 'at one', with either the divine, the universe, or both. These experiences of 'oneness' often involve the transcendence of ego or self, as if the self entirely disappears. For example the Upanishads say 'tat tvam asi', (literally, 'that thou art') meaning that all is one, Brahman, Absolute Reality.

c) Encounter with the divine

Many mystical experiences involve an encounter or union with the divine. St Teresa of Avila, for example, wrote:

> *'I used unexpectedly to experience a consciousness of the presence of God, of such a kind that I could not possibly doubt that He was within me or that I was wholly engulfed by Him*[5]

The Rajput princess and famous Hindu mystic Mirabai writes: 'I went to the root of things and found nothing but Him alone'.

Research task

Choose at least three of the following Christian Mystics and discover what they experienced:

Hildegard of Bingen

Meister Eckhart

Julian of Norwich

Teresa of Avila

John of the Cross

Teresa of Lisieux

Caroline Franks Davis in her book *The Evidential Force of Religious Experience* has a slightly different list, which includes 'mystical' and 'regenerative' but adds the following:

Interpretive: Any experience (such as the appreciation of a natural scene) which is *interpreted* in a religious way.

Quasi-sensory: an experience which appears to come to the recipient through one of the five senses. Examples include visions, voices, smells, (e.g. the smell of flowers often accompanies religious experiences), tastes, feeling of movement (e.g. travelling down a tunnel or rising above one's body).

Revelatory: The receipt of new knowledge, insight or conviction. The Prophets of the Hebrew Bible are good examples of people who had such experiences. The Zen Buddhist experience of satori (enlightenment) is another example. This involves the sudden intuitive understanding of reality as it really is (or truth) which is beyond words.

Numinous: The word numinous means the sacred or holy. The term was coined by Rudolf Otto, who described in his book *Das Heilige* 1917 (*The Idea of the Holy*) that the numen (Latin for holy) was a *mysterium tremendum* and *mysterium fascinans*, i.e. a power that is both awesome and frightening, and yet attractive. Otto argued that the experience of this power was at the heart of all religions, and it was non-rational; any attempt to explain its existence would fail.

Paranormal experiences

Many people claim to have had the kind of experience which cannot be verified scientifically. Examples of paranormal experience are telepathy (where thoughts are communicated directly without any words); clairvoyance (where information is received from a source often understood to be in another realm); telekinesis (the ability to change the material world, e.g. bend spoons, with the power of thought); mediumship (the ability to communicate with the dead); channeling (the possession of the body of a

---

[5] St Teresa of Avila, Life, chpt 10

medium by an entity from another realm); astral projection (travelling, but not using the physical body); and dowsing (the retrieval of otherwise unknown information through dowsing rods or pendulums).

Sometimes these experiences are understood to be entirely unrelated to religion. In fact many religions are deeply suspicious of them. The experiences are not in themselves religious [so it is important that, when responding to questions on the Synoptic paper, you understand that what should be written about is the religious experience you have studied in your A-level specifications]. However, many of the stories from the world's religions could be understood to be referring to these powers. For example, the Buddha gained the power to see his own and other people's past lives (is this clairvoyance?); Guru Nanak and The Prophet Muhammad both made trips to another realm (astral projection?); Jesus walked on water (telekinesis?).

Characteristics of religious experiences

A question frequently raised about the types of experiences described above is 'what is it that distinguishes them from ordinary experiences?' If, for example, someone is moved by the natural world, say a beautiful view on a summer's day, is it more appropriate to call this an *aesthetic* experience rather than a religious experience – even if that experience involves them feeling great joy, a sense of gratitude, sacredness and oneness with the natural world?

Similarly, it could be asked, 'Is the experience of telepathy a religious experience?' If such an experience were proof that the world is not quite as science currently says it is, that is very interesting indeed but, many would argue, it says nothing whatever about religion.

Writing task

1. Make a list of experiences that some people might describe as religious, but others might describe as aesthetic or paranormal.

2. From what you have read and studied so far, make a list of the characteristics you think a religious experience would have.

William James introduced a list of four characteristics that in his view a Mystical Experience would have (note that not all religious experiences are mystical):

Ineffable - it can't be described; it is beyond words; it can only be experienced;

Noetic - it gives the recipient important new knowledge, a realization of the truth and/or about how they should live their lives;

Transient - the experience itself is short-lived; it doesn't go on for long;

Passivity - it comes to the recipient from the outside; it is 'given'; it is not 'created' or 'induced'.

Numerous questions arise from James's four characteristics:

- Are all religious experiences 'ineffable', not just mystical experiences? In fact, Caroline Franks Davis argues all experiences are ineffable. Is it, for example, really possible to fully describe the taste of an orange, or the feeling of a kiss? Are not these experiences also 'ineffable'?

- What can be said about the 'knowledge' that is imparted to those who have a mystical experience (noesis)? In most cases it cannot be verified or falsified, so can it genuinely be said to be knowledge?

- Religious experiences may be 'transient' (though this depends on the definition of the religious experience – some people may describe their whole lifetime's journey of faith as a religious experience) but their *effects* are not transient.

- It could be argued that some experiences are not 'passive', but are sought for. For example, the mystics who dedicate their lives to prayer and meditation, Hindu ascetics who fast or deprive themselves of sleep or perform other austerities, or the Whirling Dervishes of the Sufi tradition who induce trance states through dancing, could all be said to be actively seeking mystical experience, so they are not passive. In response to that, however, it could be argued that the experience is still passive, because it comes to the recipient from the outside, and all they have done is made themselves ready for it.

Whirling dervishes

Numerous other studies have been undertaken into the features of religious experiences. One of the most famous was Raymond Moody's study of the Near Death Experience, *Life After Life*, published in 1975. As medical technology has advanced and more people are resuscitated, and brought back from the brink of death, many report having had strange experiences when they were unconscious, not breathing and in cardiac arrest.

From a large number of case studies Moody extracted the following common features: the first, like James's features of mystical experiences, was ineffability. People reported that words could not describe what they had experienced. They would hear the news that they had died – a nurse saying 'we're losing her' or something similar. They would experience feelings of peace and quiet, or alternatively a dramatic noise, associated with travelling down a dark tunnel. There would be an 'out of the body' experience (OBE), where they would experience themselves looking down on their body and the activities around their bed. They would encounter deceased relatives (in some cases relatives they didn't know were in fact deceased at that moment) and often have conversations in which the deceased would urge them to return to their life because they were needed.

Accounts often referred to an encounter with a 'Being of Light', who was described according to the religious background of the person (i.e. for a Protestant, it would be Jesus; for a Roman Catholic it might be Mary; for a Buddhist, the Buddha; for an agnostic, just a 'being of light').

Many experienced a 'life review' – seeing their whole life played at high speed. They often came to some kind of border or limit, which could be a stream or a wall that could not be crossed, and then returned to their bodies and were resuscitated. After the experience, some discover they can accurately report what medical procedures were carried out whilst they were unconscious and could not physically see anything. Furthermore, the impact of such an experience on the rest of the life of the experiencer can be profound. Many report a decreased fear of death, a greater sense of moral responsibility, and an increased sense of purpose and meaning in life.

In fact, by and large, religious experiences in general are joyful occurrences, which bring to their recipients a sense of serenity and peace, assuredness that 'all is well'. Some, however, are negative. Marete Jacobsen in her paper *Negative Religious Experiences: Encounters with Evil* (published by the Religious Experience Research Centre in 1999) explores experiences of hell, evil spirits and horrific visions. These tend to leave recipients very frightened.

Fruits

One important way that it might be possible to distinguish religious experience from other kinds of experience is by reference to the 'fruits' or effects of the experience in the person's life. William James, in his *Varieties of Religious Experience*, 1902, argues that an experience is 'valid' (i.e. true) if it has fruits. James came from the philosophical school of 'pragmatism', which describes the meaning of things in the world according to their function. A piece of paper is a piece of paper because it can be written on (not because it has particular properties). Thus, an experience is religious when it has the effect of transforming a person's life — when it has *fruits*.

We have already noted some of the effects that a near death experience is reported to have. Many of those who have submitted accounts of experiences to the Alister Hardy Archive claim that their lives are changed for the better after the experience. We can see the transformative effects of an experience in some of the well-known accounts from the world's religions. Take, for example, the experience of Paul on the road to

Damascus reported in Acts 9 1-30, in which he was blinded, and heard the voice of the risen Christ. The effect of this experience was to completely change the course of his life. He had been a persecutor of Christians prior to the experience. As a result ('fruit') of it, he became a Christian, an Apostle, and the founder of the Christian Church.

Another example is the historical Buddha. He lived a life of luxury, with every desire met. As a consequence of 'the four sights' he pursued an ascetic path, which eventually led to his experience of enlightenment under the Bodhi tree. This experience was so profoundly life-changing, he spent the rest of his life, until the age of 80, as an itinerant religious teacher.

Yet another example is Guru Nanak, who disappeared whilst bathing and returned three days later, claiming to have been to the Court of God, where he had received a special commission to teach God's path. He too became an itinerant teacher, travelling vast distances, founded a community of Sikhs (disciples), and preached equality.

William James argues that the marked changes in the values, lifestyle, and commitments of these people demonstrate the validity of their experience.

Writing tasks

a) One of the most famous classifications of characteristics of religious experience is that of William James, in The Varieties of Religious Experience, 1902

Ineffability: they cannot be adequately described

Noesis: they impart a new sense of knowledge

Transiency: they are short-lived

Passivity: they come as if from outside

How useful is each of these elements for an understanding of religious experience in any religion you have studied?

Evaluate the importance of personal 'experience' – as opposed to received tradition – in any religion you have studied.

b) Read the following account of a religious experience, and write short notes on its features. Amongst these you should consider James 'four characteristics' and the question of 'fruits'.

'I find it difficult to describe my experience, only to say that it seems outside of me and enormous and yet at the same time I am part of it, everything is. It is purely personal and helps me to live and love others. It is difficult to describe, but in some way because of this feeling I feel united to all people, to all living things. Of recent years the feeling has become so strong that I am now training to become a social worker because I find that I must help people: in some way I feel their unhappiness as my own.'

Religious Experience Research Centre Account no. 663, quoted in Marianne Rankin, *An Introduction to Religious Experience*, Lampeter, Religious Experience Research Centre 2005.

Problems with Religious Experiences

Those who have had a religious experience are convinced that they have experienced something real. Arjuna, when Krishna reveals himself in Chapter 11 of the Bhagavad Gita, is convinced that he sees the Absolute, Brahman. St Paul is convinced on the Damascus road that he hears the voice of the risen Christ. The person who has a near death experience is convinced that there is life after death. The mystic who experiences in prayer an overwhelming sense of love and forgiveness, is convinced of the truth of God's unconditional love.

The conviction of these individuals is perhaps understandable, but what are the rest of us to make of these experiences? What do they prove? If they were all experiences of something real, that would mean all the religions in the world were true. Is that possible? The Yorkshire Ripper reported that he heard the voice of God telling him to punish the young women that he killed. Was his experience of something real?

One problem with religious experience is that it is subjective. It rarely happens to more than one individual at a time, therefore it is not verifiable.

Verification and falsification: Flew and Ayer

The philosopher A J Ayer argued that statements or propositions could be 'verified' as true by pointing to evidence. Many statements which are 'true' do not have a great deal of strong evidence. These rely on 'weak verification'. For example, the statement 'Llewelyn the Great died in 1240' is difficult to verify, as there is no 'direct' evidence (i.e. no witnesses), but the history books do all tend to suggest it, so we can say it's true on the basis of 'weak verification'. It is however very difficult to verify an individual's subjective religious experience, even weakly.

Furthermore, statements about religious experience are also unscientific because they are unfalsifiable. For the philosopher Anthony Flew, it makes no sense to say for example 'God watches over me', because if I believe it, I won't allow any evidence to the contrary to count. So if I fall down a hole, then my interpretation is not that 'I was wrong, God is *not* watching over me', but that 'it is part of God's plan for me to fall down a hole'.

A truly logical and scientific statement has to be falsifiable. Religious language is not falsifiable, and it is often not possible to falsify a description of a religious experience.

In response to this problem of the subjectivity (and therefore unfalsifiablity and unverifiability) of religious experience, the philosopher Richard Swinburne proposes the Principle of Credulity:

'It is a principle of rationality that (in the absence of special considerations) if it seems…to a subject that x is present, then probably x is present: what one seems to perceive is probably so.[6]

In simple language, this means it is fair to assume that if someone says they see or experience something, unless there are very good reasons for thinking they might be wrong (for example they have taken a hallucinatory drug) then they probably have.

Writing task

Make a list of what Swinburne might describe as 'special considerations'.

Caroline Franks Davis argues that there are three categories of challenges to the idea that a reported experience actually proves something:

1 Description-related challenges

Since experiences happen to individuals, we are completely reliant on their descriptions of what happened to them. According to Franks Davis we should be suspicious of any description which is inconsistent with itself. This could, for example, be a description which substantially changes when it is re-told. She argues that we should also be suspicious if the behaviour of someone is not consistent with what they say they've experienced, and that we should be suspicious if the experience is not consistent with our knowledge about the world. She gives the example of Mary, who says she has seen a Dodo. We have, says Franks Davis, more reason to believe that Mary is lying, or that she does not understand the term 'dodo', than that dodos are not extinct after all.

2 Subject-related challenges

The 'subject' is the person who has the experience. If we have doubts about the honesty or stability of the person who claims to have had an experience, we should be suspicious of the description. If we think the person has been brainwashed, drugged or hypnotized, or if they are a known liar or prone to exaggeration, we have good reason to doubt what they report.

3 Object-related challenges

If we have doubts that the 'thing' that the person claims to have experienced exists, we should be suspicious. This is a difficult challenge to make, because people's ideas about what exists (e.g. God, Angels etc.) vary.

Religious and cultural background

Some philosophers, for example, George Lindbeck and Steven Katz, argue that it is not rational to see religious experiences as proof of the existence of the religious object (God, the afterlife etc.). People have these experiences because they already believe in, or at least have the concept of, God or life after death. As such they are *culturally pre-determined* to have these experiences, or at least to interpret them the way that they do. For example, in a near death experience, or a religious vision, people of Christian or even secular Western backgrounds are likely to see God, Jesus or Angels. Hindus are

---

[6] Swinburne, Richard, *The Existence of God*, Oxford, Clarendon Press, 1979 p254

likely to see Krishna or Rama. Protestants don't often see Mary, and Christians never see the prophet Muhammad.

John Wisdom's metaphor of the garden forms part of a complex discussion of the philosophy of religion, which is helpful when considering religious experience. The person who thinks there must be a gardener experiences the garden in a positive way. The person who believes in God, it could be argued, experiences the world in a positive way. They may experience awe and wonder at the natural world and the human body. They may have experiences which confirm a sense of peace and order and meaning. These people are likely to be convinced that God exists. The person who does not believe in God experiences the world in a negative way: they see disorder, chaos, confusion and pain.

Objectively speaking, it could be argued that the world offers us all this information. Our interpretation of it depends entirely on our *experience* of it. We cannot say which person in Wisdom's Garden has the correct interpretation of their experience.

Whilst it is indeed the case that people frequently experience the things they are culturally predisposed to experience, sometimes there are reports of religious experiences which lie outside of the individual's expectation or worldview. For example, the persecutor of Christians, Saul, (later Paul) would not have expected to hear the voice of the Risen Christ, leading to his conversion (though of course it could be argued that he at least had the concept of 'Christ', since he persecuted Christians).

Are religious people mad?

Sigmund Freud famously argued that religion was a 'universal, obsessional neurosis' and religious experience (what he called the 'Oceanic Experience') was nothing more than the expression of the desire to retreat from the world back into the womb. Features of religious experience, such as a sense of comfort, security, certainty, being enveloped in unconditional love and being 'at one' with the universe, he described as the experience of being in the womb. Religious people who sought that kind of experience were really wanting to 'regress' – to return to an infantile state and not face reality.

Freud and other writers have questioned the psychological health of people who see visions, have life changing experiences they can't explain, and believe in unverifiable propositions.

However, many of Freud's basic arguments have since been discredited. He argued, for instance, that the reason why people in the West believe in an omnipotent male God is because the whole culture suffers from an inherited, universal Oedipus Complex. This theory is not now regarded as tenable. Furthermore, many studies, such as those by Michael Argyle and others, show that people who have religious experiences are likely to be psychologically very well-balanced, healthy and optimistic people.

Sadhu performing austerities

Another angle from which to address the question of religious experience and psychological health is to point out that 'psychological health' is a concept which varies from culture to culture. For instance, in India, the great religious heroes, the sadhus, engage in activities such as fasting almost to the point of death, depriving themselves of sleep, living outdoors, going naked, covering themselves in ashes from funeral pyres, mortifying their bodies in all sorts of ways.

If a person were to engage in any of these activities in a western cultural setting, they would probably be considered to be mentally ill. This fact shows us that understandings of 'mental health' are culturally constructed. Not only are sadhus in India not considered to be mentally ill, they are considered to be individuals manifesting the greatest spiritual development and having attained the highest religious experiences.

Some writers, such as Susan Blackmore, argue that there are 'naturalistic' explanations of religious experiences. They are real experiences, but they can be explained by psychological or physical factors and do not require religious explanations. For example, the near death experience in her view is caused by the chemical effects of the brain losing oxygen, combined with the drugs given to patients in critical conditions and the effects of stress.

Other writers respond that whilst some of the features could be explained in this way, not all of them can be. The debate continues.

Despite all these problems of verification Marianne Rankin writes:
> *'Religious experiences, however they are interpreted, cannot simply be ignored. They are too widespread to be disregarded as the delusions of a few feeble minded individuals. Their effects are too transformative for them to be dismissed as irrelevant. Through these experiences, a spiritual or higher realm seems to enter human consciousness ...*
> *If religious experiences are indeed intimations of a greater reality, a spiritual dimension, which is reflected in the religious tradition of the world, then they are some of the most important events in human history.'* [7]

[7]Marianne Rankin *Introduction to Religious Experience*, Lampeter, RERC Occasional Paper series 3, no 2, p58

Questions and Outline Answers

Question 1

> (a) Examine the diversity of religious experience.
> (b) Determine how far religious experience can be regarded as a reliable guide to an understanding of God.

Answer

This question requires you to show knowledge and understanding of various forms of religious experience from at least two different areas of study (until 2010) and be able to assess the significance of such experience for a religious believer's understanding of God.

In your answer to part (a) you would demonstrate your knowledge and understanding of different types or features of religious experience, from two distinct areas of study. For high marks (levels 4 and 5) you would have to describe at least three types or features and illustrate them. You might chose: mystical, paranormal, charismatic, regenerative, conversion, feelings of awe and wonder, sense of oneness with the universe or with the divine, sense of overwhelming love, communication with a personal god, experience of liberation, moksha or nirvana, realization of a new truth, sense of joy and release.

In your answer to part (b) you might argue that personal religious experience is an important locus of authority in most religions and that most religions are founded on the religious experience of their founders. Personal religious experience can be dramatic, taking the form of revelation, resulting in total conviction, not only for the individual who receives it (e.g. impact of the Prophets in the Hebrew Bible). It might be less dramatic, like the experience of communal worship or meditation and simply confirm beliefs about God. On the other hand you might argue that religious experiences are not verifiable or falsifiable. There has been no overwhelmingly conclusive near death experience accepted by all scientists, for example. Some people argue that religious experiences can be explained naturalistically. You might mention that not all religions believe in God, yet they still have religious experience. You must show more than one point of view, and attempt to come to a reasoned conclusion. You will be awarded a maximum of level 3 (just over half marks) if you present a one-sided response.

Question 2

> (a) Examine some individual and some shared aspects of religious experiences.
> (b) 'Religious experiences are simply misinterpretations of natural experiences.' Evaluate the validity of this statement.

Answer

This question requires you to show knowledge and understanding of some individual and some shared aspects of religious experience from at least two different areas of study (until 2010) and be able to assess whether religious experiences are no more than a subjective misunderstanding of normal experience.

In your answer to part (a) you would refer to forms of individual religious experience such as mysticism, conversion, personal prayer, sense of awe and wonder, of inner peace/and or release. Communal forms include institutional worship, religious rites of passage, mass pilgrimage, and so on. Some forms (e.g. charismatic and paranormal phenomena) may be in either category depending on the aspects presented. Your answer should draw on at least two areas of study, and you would only receive a maximum of level 3 (just over half marks) if you concentrate on either 'individual' or 'communal' and didn't focus on both.

In your answer to part (b) you might argue that religious experiences are subjective and cannot be verified or falsified. Very often religious experiences actually seem to be the symptoms of mental illness. Experiences described as religious have often been induced by hypnosis or drugs. Experiences can also be described as the effects of 'wishful thinking'. But on the other hand, religious experiences can be understood as self-authenticating either in themselves or by reference to 'fruits'. They are often consistent with other knowledge within a tradition. The patterns found within them contribute to a cumulative case for their veracity. On the principle of credulity they can be accepted as described, unless a there is a good reason for not doing so.

You must show more than one point of view, and attempt to come to a reasoned conclusion. You will be awarded a maximum of level 3 (just over half marks) if you present a one-sided response.

Question 3

(a) Describe and illustrate different features of religious experience.
(b) Critically examine the view that an individual's religious commitment depends mainly on personal religious experience.

Answer

This question requires you to show knowledge and understanding of features of religious experience from at least two different areas of study (until 2010) and be able to evaluate whether or not personal religious experience is paramount in determining individual's religious commitment.

In your answer to part (a) you would demonstrate your knowledge and understanding of different features of religious experience, from at least two distinct areas of study. For high marks (levels 4 and 5) you would have to describe at least three features and illustrate them. You might choose: features of mystical, paranormal, charismatic, near death, regenerative, or conversion experiences; feelings of awe and wonder, sense of oneness with the universe or with the divine, sense of overwhelming love, communication with a personal god, experience of liberation, moksha or nirvana, realization of a new truth, sense of joy and release. High scoring candidates would mention James' Four Characteristics of Mystical States (transiency, ineffability, passivity, noetic quality).

In your answer to part (b) you might argue that without personal religious experience a commitment would be hard to make. Experience carries with it conviction. The most famous figures in religions are distinctive because of their personal religious experiences (e.g. St Paul, the Buddha, Arjuna, Moses, Muhammad). Personal religious experience carries great authority. On the other hand it could be argued that other sources of authority are more important, such as creeds or scriptures, or institutions, or cultural background. Also sometimes those who have had strong religious experiences actually leave or challenge the institution to which they have had a commitment. You must show more than one point of view, and attempt to come to a reasoned conclusion. You will be awarded a maximum of level 3 (just over half marks) if you present a one-sided response.

Glossary

Alister Hardy	Marine biologist and Darwinian Evolutionist, who founded the Religious Experience Research Unit in 1969 to study the universal human phenomenon of religious experience
charismatic	An experience (usually Christian) of receipt of 'gifts of the spirit' e.g. healing, prophecy, speaking in tongues
conversion	Turning from no religion, or another religion, to a new religion. Conversions frequently occur as the result of religious experience
falsification	The argument that for a statement to be acceptable in scientific terms, it must be open to being proved false
ineffable	It cannot be described and is beyond words. One of William James's Four Characteristics of Mystical Experience
mysticism	The experience of a direct encounter with God. May also be understood as the experience of loss of ego or self, and unity with the divine or with the universe
near death experience	Experience with a set of common features had by those in cardiac failure or otherwise very near death, which confirms (for the experiencer) the survival of the individual beyond death
noetic	Gives new knowledge. One of William James's Four Characteristics of Mystical Experience
numinous	'holy', 'sacred' a word coined by Rudolf Otto
out of body experience	An experience of leaving the body, which confirms for the experiencer that they are more than just their body
paranormal	Something which cannot currently be explained scientifically
passive	'Comes to the recipient from the outside.' One of William James's Four Characteristics of Mystical Experience
psychedelic	'mind-opening'
psychic experience	Experience which is beyond the physical (but not necessarily the same as 'religious experience')
regenerative	An experience which gives new life or meaning to a person
Religious Experience Research Centre	Founded in 1969 in Oxford by Sir Alister Hardy, now at the University of Wales, Lampeter. The world's most prestigious research centre for the study of religious experience
revelation	A communication from the divine, or the realisation of a profound truth
Rudolf Otto	1869-1937 author of *Das Heilige* (*The Idea of the Holy*) 1917, a seminal work about the numinous experience

sacred	Holy, 'the other'
transcendent	Above and beyond, outside of human categories
transient	Of short duration. One of William James's Four Characteristics of Mystical Experience
unitive	An experience which confirms the unity of all things, or the unity of all things with the divine
verification	The argument that for a statement to acceptable in scientific terms there must be evidence to support it
weak verification	The principle on which a statement is accepted as true, even though the evidence for it is weak.
William James	1842-1910 author of *The Varieties of Religious Experience*, a seminal study of individual religious experience

Select Bibliography

For information and a list of publications from the Religious Experience Research Centre, see **www.alisterhardytrust.org.uk**, or contact
The Librarian, Religious Experience Research Centre,
University of Wales, Lampeter, Ceredigion, SA48 7ED.

Badham, Paul, *Religious and Near Death experience in Relation to Belief in a Future Life*, Occasional Paper 13, Religious Experience Research Centre, University of Wales, Lampeter, 1997

Donovan, Peter, *Interpreting Religious Experience*, Oxford, Religious Experience Research Centre, 1988

Fox, Mark, *Religion Spirituality and the Near Death Experience*, London, Routledge, 2003

Franks Davis, Caroline *The Evidential Force of Religious Experience*, Oxford, Oxford University Press, 1989

Hardy, Alister, *The Spiritual Nature of Man*, Oxford, Oxford University Press, 1979

Hay, David, *Exploring Inner Space*, Oxford, Mowbray, 1987

Hay, David, *Religious Experience Today*, London, Mowbray, 1990

James, William, *The Varieties of Religious Experience*, New York Longman, 1902 (many reprints)

Maxwell, Meg, & Tschudin, Verena, *Seeing the Invisible, Modern Religious and other Transcendent Experiences*, Oxford, Religious Experience Research Centre, 1996

Momen, Moojan, *The Phenomenon of Religion: A Thematic Approach*, Oxford, Oneworld, 1999, Chapter 4

Otto, Rudolf, *The Idea of the Holy*, Harmondsworth, Penguin, 1917

Rankin, Marianne *An Introduction to Religious Experience*, Occasional Paper 2 (3rd Series) Religious Experience Research Centre, University of Wales, Lampeter, 2005

Smart, Ninian *The World's Religions: Old Traditions and Modern Transformations*, Cambridge, Cambridge University Press, 1989

Webber, Jonathan, *Revelation and Religious Experience*, London, Abacus, 1995